CLASSIC QUOTES ABOUT
DOGS

When a man's best friend is his
dog, that dog has a problem.

EDWARD ABBEY

Dogs feel very strongly that they should
always go with you in the car, in case
the need should arise for them to bark
violently at nothing right in your ear.

DAVE BARRY

Dogs need to sniff the ground; it's how
they keep abreast of current events. The
ground is a giant dog newspaper, containing
all kinds of late-breaking dog news items,
which, if they are especially urgent, are
often continued in the next yard.

DAVE BARRY

A dog teaches a boy fidelity, perseverance, and to turn around three times before lying down.

ROBERT BENCHLEY

A dog is the only thing on earth that loves you more than he loves himself.

JOSH BILLINGS

You enter into a certain amount of madness when you marry a person with pets.

NORA EPHRON

We give dogs time we can spare, space we can spare, and love we can spare. And in return, dogs give us their all. It's the best deal man has ever made.

MARGERY FACKLAM

Dogs love their friends and bite their enemies, quite unlike people, who are incapable of pure love and always have to mix love and hate.

SIGMUND FREUD

Women and cats will do as they please, and men and dogs should relax and get used to the idea.

ROBERT A. HEINLEIN

Whoever said you can't buy happiness forgot about puppies.

GENE HILL

To his dog, every man is Napoleon; hence the constant popularity of dogs.

ALDOUS HUXLEY

Man is a dog's idea of what God should be.

HOLBROOK JACKSON

Anybody who doesn't know what soap tastes like never washed a dog.

FRANKLIN P. JONES

"You drank the waterbed!"

Don't accept your dog's admiration as conclusive evidence that you are wonderful.

ANN LANDERS

No animal should ever jump up on the dining room furniture unless absolutely certain that he can hold his own in the conversation.

FRAN LEIBOWITZ

Outside of a dog, a book is probably man's best friend; inside of a dog, it's too dark to read.

GROUCHO MARX

No one appreciates the very special genius of your conversation as the dog does.

CHRISTOPHER MORLEY

Did you ever walk into a room and forget why you walked in? I think that's how dogs spend their lives.

SUE MURPHY

"I'm having second thoughts
about our new watchdog."

The average dog is a nicer person
than the average person.

ANDY ROONEY

I wonder if other dogs think poodles are
members of a weird religious cult.

RITA RUDNER

I loathe people who keep dogs. They
are cowards who haven't got the
guts to bite people themselves.

AUGUST STRINDBERG

If I have any beliefs about immortality, it
is that certain dogs I have known will go
to heaven, and very, very few persons.

JAMES THURBER

If you pick up a starving dog and make him
prosperous, he will not bite you; that is the
principal difference between a dog and a man.

MARK TWAIN

Ever consider what they must think of us? I mean, here we come back from a grocery store with the most amazing haul—chicken, pork, half a cow. They must think we're the greatest hunters on earth!

ANNE TYLER

My dog is worried about the economy because Alpo is up to $3 a can. That's almost $21 in dog money.

JOE WEINSTEIN

I've seen a look in dogs' eyes, a quickly vanishing look of amazed contempt, and I am convinced that basically dogs think humans are nuts.

JOHN STEINBECK

Say something idiotic and nobody but a dog politely wags his tail.

VIRGINIA GRAHAM

"I've always been *good,*
but I never felt I was a *Great* Dane."

All knowledge, the totality of all questions
and answers, is contained in the dog.

FRANZ KAFKA

My neighbor has two dogs. One of
them says to the other, "Woof!"
The other replies, "Moo!"
The first dog is perplexed. "Moo?
Why did you say, 'Moo'?"
The other dog says, "I'm trying to
learn a foreign language."

MOREY AMSTERDAM

Life is like a dogsled team. If you ain't the
lead dog, the scenery never changes.

LEWIS GRIZZARD

There are three faithful friends—an old
wife, an old dog, and ready money.

BEN FRANKLIN

The other day I saw two dogs walk over to a parking meter. One of them says to the other, "How do you like that? Pay toilets!"

DAVE STARR

I went to an exclusive kennel club. It was very exclusive. There was a sign out front: No Dogs Allowed.

PHIL FOSTER

He that lieth down with dogs shall rise up with fleas.

BEN FRANKLIN

I have a great dog. She's half Lab, half pit bull. A good combination. Sure, she might bite off my leg, but she'll bring it back to me.

JIM CELESTE

Don't make the mistake of treating your dogs like humans, or they'll treat you like dogs.

MARTHA SCOTT

"I saw two illegal ewe-turns."

When you leave your dogs in the morning,
they stick their nose in the door crack
and stand there like a portrait until
you turn the key eight hours later.

ERMA BOMBECK

Every time I go near the stove,
the dog howls.

PHILLIS DILLER

My advice to any diplomat who
wants to have good press is to have
two or three kids and a dog.

CARL ROWAN

Oh, that dog! Ever hear of a German
shepherd that bites its nails? Barks with
a lisp? You say, "Attack!" and he has
one. All he does is piddle. He's nothing
but a fur-covered kidney that barks.

PHYLLIS DILLER

I've been on so many blind dates,
I should get a free dog.

WENDY LIEBMAN

I bought my grandmother a Seeing Eye
dog. But he's a little sadistic. He does
impressions of cars screeching to a halt.

LARRY AMOROS

I like driving around with my two dogs,
especially on the freeways. I make them wear
little hats so I can use the car-pool lanes.

MONICA PIPER

Keep running after a dog, and
he will never bite you.

FRANÇOIS RABELAIS

I am sir Oracle, and when I open
my lips, let no dog bark.

WILLIAM SHAKESPEARE

About the only thing on a farm that
has an easy time is the dog.

EDGAR WATSON HOWE

The more I see of the depressing stature
of people, the more I admire my dogs.

ALPHONSE DE LAMARTINE

Revenge is often like biting a dog
because the dog bit you.

AUSTIN O'MALLEY

Histories are more full of examples of
the fidelity of dogs than of friends.

ALEXANDER POPE

Man is an animal that makes bargains.
No other animal does this—no dog
exchanges bones with another.

ADAM SMITH

"It certainly *is* an emergency—
he swallowed my *credit card*!"

CRAZY CROSSBREEDS

Question: What do you get when you cross a pointer with a setter?

Answer: *A poinsetter, a traditional Christmas pet.*

Question: What do you get when you cross a Kerry blue terrier with a Skye terrier?

Answer: *A blue Skye, a dog for visionaries.*

Question: What do you get when you cross an Irish water spaniel with an English springer spaniel?

Answer: *An Irish springer, a dog that's fresh and clean as a whistle.*

Question: What do you get when you cross a Labrador retriever with a curly-coated retriever?

Answer: *A Lab-coat retriever, the choice of research scientists.*

"Can't you just feed him less?"

Question: What do you get when you cross a Newfoundland with a basset hound?

Answer: *A newfound asset hound, a dog for financial advisors.*

Question: What do you get when you cross a terrier with a bulldog?

Answer: *A terribull, a dog prone to awful mistakes.*

Question: What do you get when you cross a bloodhound with a Labrador?

Answer: *A blabador, a dog that barks incessantly.*

Question: What do you get when you cross a malamute with a pointer?

Answer: *A mute point, owned by…oh well, it doesn't matter anyway.*

Question: What do you get when you cross a collie with a malamute?

Answer: *A commute, a dog that travels to work.*

Question: What do you get when you cross a deerhound with a terrier?

Answer: *A derriere, a dog that's true to the end.*

Joe Cocker Spaniel

Question: What do you get when you cross a collie and a Lhasa apso?

Answer: *A collapso, a dog that folds up for easy transport.*

Question: What do you get if you cross a skunk with a big dog?

Answer: *A scent bernard.*

Question: What would you get if you crossed a newt and a poodle?

Answer: *A newdle.*

Question: What would you get if you crossed a pit bull with Lassie?

Answer: *A dog that bites your leg off and then runs for help.*

Question: What do you get when you cross a black dog and a white dog?

Answer: *A greyhound.*

Question: What do you get when you cross a Cocker spaniel and a steer?

Answer: *A cocker-and-bull story.*

Question: What do you get if you cross a dog with a blind mole?

Answer: *A dog that keeps barking up the wrong tree.*

Question: What do you get if you cross a sheepdog with Jell-O?

Answer: *The collie wobbles.*

Question: What do you get if you cross a rottweiller and a hyena?

Answer: *I don't know, but I'll join in if it laughs!*

Question: What do you get when you cross a poodle with a chicken?

Answer: *Pooched eggs.*

Question: What do you get when you cross a poodle, a cocker spaniel, and a rooster?

Answer: *A cocka-poodle-doo!*

Question: What do you get if you cross a dog and a cheetah?

Answer: *A dog that chases cars—and catches them.*

"I'm a newshound, Curt."

Question: What do you get if you cross a giraffe with a dog?

Answer: *An animal that barks at low-flying aircraft.*

Question: What do you get if you cross a dog with an airliner?

Answer: *A jet-setter.*

Question: What do you get when you cross a small dog and a large boat?

Answer: *A ship tzu.*

Question: What do you get if you cross a sheepdog with a rose?

Answer: *A collie-flower.*

Question: What do you get if you cross a yellow dog with a phone?

Answer: *A golden receiver!*

Question: What do you get when you cross a dog with a sprinter?

Answer: *The 100-yard dachshund.*

Question: What do you get when you cross a
  dog with a journalist?

Answer: *A rover reporting.*

Question: What do you get when a cantaloupe
  and a dog have a pup?

Answer: *A melon-collie baby.*

Question: What do you get when you cross a
  dog with an owl?

Answer: *Whoo-curs?*

Question: What do you get when you cross a
  Doberman with a saber-toothed tiger?

Answer: *A very nervous mailman.*

Question: What would you get if you crossed a
  puppy with a very mean boy?

Answer: *A bully dog.*

Help Wanted

A local business was looking for office help. A sign in the window said, "Help wanted. Must be able to type, must be good with a computer, and must be bilingual. We are an equal opportunity employer."

A short time afterward, a dog trotted up to the window, saw the sign, and went inside. He looked at the receptionist and wagged his tail, and then he walked over to the sign, looked at it, and whined.

Getting the idea, the receptionist got the office manager. The office manager looked at the dog and was surprised to say the least. However, the dog looked determined, so she led him into the office. Inside, the dog jumped up on the chair and stared at her.

She said, "I can't hire you. The sign says you have to be able to type." The dog jumped down, went to the computer, and proceeded to type out a perfect letter. He printed the page, trotted over to the office manager, gave it to her, and jumped back on the chair.

She was stunned, but she told the dog, "The sign says you have to be good with a computer." The dog jumped down again and returned to the computer. He proceeded to demonstrate his expertise with various programs and produced a sample spreadsheet and database and presented them to the office manager.

By this time she was totally dumbfounded! She looked at the dog and said, "I realize that you are a very intelligent dog and have some interesting abilities. However, I still can't give you the job." The dog jumped down, went to a copy of the sign, and put his paw on the sentence about being an equal opportunity employer.

The office manager said, "Yes, but the sign also says that you have to be bilingual."

The dog looked at her straight in the face and said, "Meow."

How Many Dogs Does It Take to Change a Lightbulb?

Golden retriever: The sun is shining, the day is young, we've got our whole lives ahead of us, and you're inside worrying about a stupid burned-out lightbulb?

Border collie: Just one. And I'll replace any wiring that's not up to code.

Dachshund: I can't reach the stupid lamp!

Toy poodle: I'll just blow in the border collie's ear, and he'll do it. By the time he finishes rewiring the house, my nails will be dry.

Rottweiler: Go ahead—try and make me.

Shih tzu: Puh-leeze, dah-ling. Let the servants...

Lab: Oh, me, me! Pleeeeeeze let me change the lightbulb! Can I? Can I? Huh? Huh? Can I?

Malamute: Let the border collie do it. You can feed me while he's busy.

Cocker spaniel: Why change it? I can wet on the carpet in the dark.

Doberman pinscher: While it's dark, I'll guard the door.

Mastiff: Mastiffs are *not* afraid of the dark.

Hound dog: Zzzz...

Chihuahua: Yo quiero Taco Bulb.

Irish wolfhound: Can somebody else do it? I don't feels so good.

"He's in data retrieval."

Pointer: I see it—there it is, right there…

Greyhound: It isn't moving. Who cares?

Australian shepherd: Put all the lightbulbs in a little circle…

Old English sheepdog: Lightbulb? Lightbulb? That thing I just ate was a lightbulb?

Man to dog trainer: "Every time a bell rings, my dog goes into the corner."

Dog trainer: "That's OK; he's a boxer."

A wife says to her husband one weekend morning, "We've got such a clever dog. He brings in the daily newspapers every morning."

Her husband replies, "Well, lots of dogs can do that."

The wife responded, "But we've never subscribed!"

During break time at obedience school, two dogs were talking. One said to the other, "The thing I hate about obedience school is that you learn all this stuff you will never use in the real world."

"Mr. Shep is not accepting
any calls today."

"I'm afraid of needles."

A man takes his rottweiler to the vet and says, "My dog is cross-eyed. Can you do anything for him?"

The vet says, "Well, let's have a look at him." So the vet picks the dog up while examining his eyes. Finally he says, "I'm going to have to put him down."

"What? Just because he is cross-eyed?"

"No, he's just really, really heavy."

On the door of the little country store, a stranger noticed a sign: "Danger! Beware of Dog!" Inside he saw a harmless old hound dog asleep on the floor beside the cash register. He asked the store manager, "Is that the dog folks are supposed to beware of?"

"Yep, that's him," he replied.

The stranger could not help but be amused. "That certainly doesn't look like a dangerous dog to me. Why in the world would you post that sign?"

"Because," the owner replied, "before I posted that sign, people kept tripping over him."

A burglar is sneaking through a house one night when out of the darkness comes a voice: "I can see you, and so can Jesus."

The burglar freezes in his tracks and is too

frightened to move. After ten minutes, nothing has happened, so he moves forward. Again from the darkness comes the voice, "I can see you, and so can Jesus."

The burglar is petrified and too frightened to move a muscle. After 30 minutes, he decides to do something. He backs very slowly and tentatively to the wall and feels around for a light switch. He switches on the light, and there in front of him sits a cockatoo in a cage, who says, "I can see you, and so can Jesus."

Greatly relieved, the burglar sighs, "It's just a cocky."

The cocky looks at the burglar and says, "I might be just a cocky, but Jesus is a big German shepherd."

🐾 🐾 🐾

A veterinarian was sick and went to see a doctor. The doctor asked him all the usual questions about symptoms, but the vet interrupted him: "Hey look, I am a vet—I don't need to ask my patients all these questions. I can tell what is wrong just by looking. Can't you?"

The doctor nodded, stood back, looked him up and down, quickly wrote out a prescription, handed it to him, and said, "There you are. Of course, if that doesn't work, we'll have to have you put down."

🐾 🐾 🐾

Reasons Not to Train a Dog

- I like to see the paw prints on my visitors' clothes.
- The house is too orderly.
- I love the sound of barking in the morning, noon, afternoon, evening, and night.
- I want the vet to get a new BMW.
- My garden and backyard need renovation, and I don't want to pay a gardener.
- My furniture looks too nice.
- My neighbors don't complain enough.
- I don't need a full night's sleep.
- My kids aren't enough of a challenge.
- I want to see if my spouse really meant those vows.

Did you ever notice that when you blow in a dog's face, he gets mad at you? But when you take him in a car, he sticks his head out the window.

How to Photograph a Puppy

1. Remove film from box and load camera.
2. Remove film box from puppy's mouth and throw in trash.

"Your best friend, Sparky,
rolled over on you."

3. Remove puppy from trash and brush coffee grounds from muzzle.

4. Choose a suitable background for photo.

5. Mount camera on tripod and focus.

6. Find puppy and take dirty sock from mouth.

7. Place puppy in prefocused spot and return to camera.

8. Forget about spot and crawl after puppy on knees.

9. Focus with one hand and fend off puppy with other hand.

10. Get tissue and clean nose print from lens.

11. Put cat outside and put peroxide on the scratch on puppy's nose.

12. Put magazines back on coffee table.

13. Try to get puppy's attention by squeaking toy over your head.

14. Replace your glasses and check camera for damage.

15. Jump up in time to grab puppy and say, "No, outside! No, outside!"

16. Call spouse to clean up the mess.

17. Sit back in La-Z-Boy and resolve to teach puppy "sit" and "stay" the first thing in the morning.

"We ought to get seven times
the gifts on our birthdays."

"Now, if I could only teach him to click."

15 Reasons Dogs Do Not Use Computers

1. Can't stick their heads out of Windows 2007.

2. Fetch command not available on all platforms.

3. Hard to read the monitor with their heads cocked to one side.

4. Too difficult to mark every website they visit.

5. Can't help attacking the screen when they hear "You've got mail."

6. Fire hydrant icon is very frustrating.

7. Involuntary tail wagging is dead giveaway they're browsing websites instead of working.

8. Keep bruising noses trying to catch that Frisbee video.

9. Not at all fooled by chuckwagon screen saver.

10. Still trying to come up with an emoticon that signifies tail-wagging.

11. Waiting for the introduction of the Microsoft Opposable Thumb.

12. Carpal paw syndrome.

13. Dogs aren't geeks! Now, cats, on the other hand…

14. Saliva-coated mouse is difficult to maneuver.

15. TrO HyAqR4tDc TgrOo TgYPmE WeIjTyH P;AzWqS,.

Ten Reasons Why It's Great to Be a Dog

1. If it itches, you can reach it. And no matter where it itches, no one will be offended if you scratch it in public.

2. No one notices if you have hair growing in weird places as you get older.

3. Personal hygiene is a blast: No one expects you to take a bath every day, and you don't even have to comb your own hair.

4. Having a wet nose is considered a sign of good health.

5. No one thinks less of you for passing gas. Some people might actually think you're cute.

6. Who needs a big home entertainment system? A bone or an old shoe can entertain you for hours.

7. You can spend hours just smelling stuff.

8. No one ever expects you to pay for lunch or dinner. You never have to worry about table manners, and if you gain weight, it's someone else's fault.

9. It doesn't take much to make you happy. You're always excited to see the same people. All they have to do is leave the room for five minutes and come back.

10. Every garbage can looks like a cold buffet to you.

"Normally, he's an indoor dog,
but he got into the bean dip."

CURIOUS DOG CONVERSATIONS

Bob: My dog took first place in the cat show.
Fred: How did he do that?
Bob: He took the cat.

Mary: Did you tell me that your dog's bark is worse than his bite?
Carrie: Yes, why?
Mary: Then don't let him bark...he just bit me.

Police officer: You are charged with having your dog chase a man on a bicycle.
Owner: That's crazy—my dog doesn't even know how to ride a bicycle.

"I'm sorry, Daisy, but you knew I was blue collar when you married me."

Buyer: Are you sure this dog you're selling me is loyal?

Seller: He sure is. I've sold him five times, and every time he's come back.

Bill: My dog is going to obedience school.

Jill: That's expensive. How can you afford it?

Bill: He won a collarship.

Pam: How do you like my new dog?

Sam: Spitz?

Pam: No, but he drools a lot.

First mailman: A dog bit me on the leg this morning.

Second mailman: Did you put anything on it?

First mailman: No, he liked it plain.

Harry: Would you like to play with our new dog?

Shari: He looks very fierce. Does he bite?

Harry: That's what I would like to find out.

"Unfortunately, there are few
things worse than his bite."

Hunter: Why does your dog have a mouthful of duck feathers?

Gunther: He's very obedient. I told him to get down.

Holly: Is that dog new?

Wally: No. He's a used cur.

"Why did you kill my dog?" demanded the dog's owner.

"Because he tried to bite me," the would-be victim replied.

"But why didn't you use the other end of the pitchfork?"

"Why didn't your dog come at me with his other end?"

The art world is amused by the legend of the animal painter who was found rubbing raw meat on a painting of a dog.

"What's the idea?" asked his friend.

"A wealthy woman is coming in this afternoon to see this painting. I happen to know she never goes out without her poodle. When her dog gets excited about this painting, she will probably buy it."

"Things are looking up."

A tourist took a cab through an upscale neighborhood and, while passing a large estate, noticed two huge dogs carved out of granite at the entrance. Hoping to have some fun with his driver, the visitor asked, "How often do they feed those big dogs?"

"Whenever they bark," said the driver.

Customer: I'm interested in a dog for my wife.

Pet shop owner: I'm sorry, sir, we don't do swaps.

Brett: I think my dalmatian has a rash.

Vet: We'd better do a spot check.

Customer: Is that pooch a good watch-dog?

Pet store owner: Absolutely. He'll raise a ruckus every time he sees a stranger.

Customer: How do I know you're not just making that up?

Pet store owner: The dog comes with a money-bark guarantee.

Judy: How did Rover make out at the pet show?

Rudy: He was a sure thing for best of breed, but at the last minute a second basset hound showed up.

Dog owner: Doctor, I've tried everything to calm Rex down, but he's still a vicious dog.

Vet: Give him onions, garlic, and limburger cheese for his meals.

Dog owner: How will that help?

Vet: His bark will be worse than his bite.

Hank: I see you got a new puppy. Does he have his papers?

Frank: Does he ever! They're all over the house.

Kim: Our pet dog is very friendly. Every time people come to visit, he wags his tail and licks their hands.

Tim: Sounds like he's a real welcome mutt.

Home buyer:	Are there any barking dogs in this neighborhood?
Real estate agent:	Oh, no. It's an extremely quiet neighborhood.
Home buyer:	That's good. I've got a couple of dogs that bark constantly, and I don't think I could stand listening to any more.

🐾 🐾 🐾

Customer:	I'd like to buy a sweater for my dog.
Salesperson:	Perhaps you could bring your dog in so we can get a proper fit.
Customer:	I can't do that. The sweater is a surprise.

🐾 🐾 🐾

Two dogs were walking down the street. One dog said, "Wait here a minute. I'll be right back."

He crossed the street, sniffed a lamppost for a while, and then walked back across the street.

The other dog asked, "What was that all about?"

"I was just checking my messages."

🐾 🐾 🐾

After many years of dedicated service, a maid was stunned to learn that her employer was dismissing her. Upon hearing of her fate, the maid took a large steak from the refrigerator and fed it to the family dog.

"What are you doing?" snapped the employer in anger.

The maid replied, "That was a reward for all of his years of service."

"What do you mean, years of service?" asked the employer.

The maid answered, "Your dog always helped me clean your dishes."

A man took his talking dog to a theatrical agent. The dog began to tell jokes in three different languages.

"What do you think?" asked the dog's owner.

The agent replied, "Well, his delivery's all right, but his material is a bit weak."

A medieval castle had been under siege for many months, and the people inside were running out of food and water. Unless help arrived soon, everyone would perish.

The king called all the knights together to

discuss the gravity of the situation. One knight offered to break out of the castle and ride for help, but the king reminded him that all of the horses had been killed.

The knight then suggested that he ride for help on the back of a huge wolfhound.

The keeper of the dogs said that would be impossible. "The wolfhound has broken its leg and can only hobble along. The only dog available is a chihuahua, and I wouldn't send a knight out on a dog like this."

Bev: Are there any wild dogs around here?
Kev: No, but I can take a tame one and irritate him for you.

A Great Dane went into an ice cream shop and ordered a two-dollar sundae. He put down a twenty-dollar bill to pay for it. The clerk thought, *What can a Great Dane know about money?* So he handed back a single dollar in change.

As he did, he said, "You know, we don't get many Great Danes in here."

"No wonder," answered the Great Dane, "at nineteen dollars a sundae."

"You're scaring the birds away."

John: What is the name of your dog?
Joan: Ginger.
John: Does Ginger bite?
Joan: No, Ginger snaps.

What we say to sled dogs: "Mush! Hike! Gee! Haw!"

What they hear: "Blah! Blah! Blah! Blah!"

First sled dog in heaven: "For 14 years I survived storms, fights with polar bears and wolves, falls into crevasses, plunges through the ice into the icy ocean…"

Second sled dog in heaven: "How did you get here?"

First sled dog in heaven: "When I was sleeping, my stupid owner ran over me with his snowmobile!"

Patient: "Doctor! I keep thinking I'm a sled dog!"

Doctor: "How long has this been going on?"

Patient: "Ever since I was a pup."

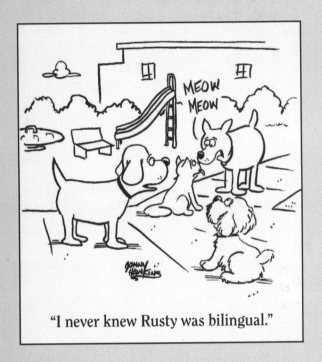

"I never knew Rusty was bilingual."

Knock-knock.
Who's there?
Detail.
Detail who?
Detail is wagging de dog.

Knock-knock.
Who's there?
Beagle.
Beagle who?
Beagle with cream cheese, please.

Knock-knock.
Who's there?
Defense.
Defense who?
Defense is what keeps de dog in de back yard.

"Now, I'm not complaining, but why is there a flea collar on my chili dog?"

Amazon—a dog with a big mouth

Ammo—a dog that has plenty of droppings

Aristotle—a very intelligent dog

Atlantis—a dog that loves the water

Axle—a dog that loves to chase cars

Bandito—a dog that loves to pillage your house and yard

Banzai—a dog that looks forward to destroying everything

Beelzebub—another name for the devil

Bobo—a slow-learning dog

Bozo—a clown dog that loves attention

Bubba—a good-old-boys' dog

Chaos—a dog that gets into everything

Chewy—a dog that destroys anything he can put in his mouth

CEO—a dog that thinks he is in charge

Caddy—a dog that loves to play fetch

Captain—a dog that is in charge of your house

Cheetah—a very fast dog

Chopper—a dog that loves to chew up everything

Colonel—another dog who thinks he is in charge of your house

Cowboy—a hard dog to tame and teach obedience

Curmudgeon—a fuddy-duddy dog

Diablo—a Spanish name for the devil

Digby—a dog that loves to dig holes all over the yard

Dodger—a dog that sneaks around and does subtle things

Dodo—a dog that has a hard time learning anything but how to eat

Doolittle—a lazy dog

Doodle—a dog that will go to the bathroom anywhere

Dynamo—a dog that is constantly on the move and full of energy

Ebony—a black dog

"Yes, about this toy poodle you sold me…"

Elvis—a dog that cries and whines a lot

Fandango—an energetic and animated dog

Frisbee—a dog that devours flying objects

Gargoyle—a dog that is a little uglier than most

Gator—a dog that makes cats disappear

Geronimo—a dog that doesn't look before it leaps

Gizmo—a dog that gets into everything with great curiosity

Gypsy—a dog that has a hard time staying home

Harley—a dog that loves to go for rides with the wind blowing in its face

Hercules—a strong dog

Hermit—a quiet and solitary dog

Hocus-Pocus—a dog that disappears a lot

Houdini—a dog that has learned lots of tricks

Igloo—a dog that wants to be outside regardless of the weather

Iris—a dog that loves to destroy your flowers

Java—a dog that loves to wake you up early in the morning

Jekyll—a moody dog

"I sentence you to 5 swats
with a rolled up newspaper."

Joker—an unpredictable dog

King—a dog that rules the family

Lazarus—a dog rescued from the dog pound

Limbo—an agile and active dog

Lollypop—a dog that is constantly licking

Loony—a dog that is completely crazy

Maverick—an out-of-control dog

Mayhem—a dog that wreaks absolute havoc in your life

Midas—a dog that can change your attitude from sadness to richness

Midnight—a dog that loves to wander late at night

Mohawk—a dog that constantly visits the dog barber

Monk—a shy, reclusive dog

Neptune—a dog that loves to dive in your swimming pool

Nitro—a highly explosive and energetic dog

Nudge—a dog that is constantly nosing around

Omega—a dog that will probably be your last one

Oreo—a black and white dog

Outlaw—a dog that is always getting into trouble and doing its own thing

Pandora—a curious dog that has no idea what it's doing

Paw—a dog that is constantly jumping on people

Pharaoh—a dog that thinks everyone should be its servant

Poco—a small dog

Pogo—a dog that jumps up and down a lot

Presto—a dog that disappears all the time

Queenie—a dog that thinks she is on the throne

Quirk—a dog with strange and weird tendencies

Ragtime—a dog that loves to tear up clothes and shoes

Rebel—a dog that will not come to you when you call

Ringo—a long-haired dog

Rogue—a dog that seems to be a prankster

Sabertooth—a good guard dog

Sahara—a dog that loves to lay in the sun

"We shoulda never named her 'Queen'."

Scooter—a dog that loves to chase motorcycles and bikes

Scrappy—a dog that fights with other dogs

Sergeant—a dog that protects the family

Sherlock—a curious dog

Stinky—a dog with bad breath or that passes gas

Sumo—a dog that is a little overweight

Tag—a dog that always thinks he's it and chases you

Tarzan—a dog that can turn your house into a jungle

Tempest—a dog with an attitude

Tipsy—a clumsy dog

Tornado—a dog that rips up everything in its path

Tumbleweed—a dog that loves to roll on the grass

Utopia—a dog that is oblivious to any problems

Vagabond—a dog that loves to wander

Van Gogh—a dog with a damaged ear

Velcro—a dog that never leaves your side

The frustrating thing for Stanley
was that it was *his* dog.

Voodoo—a dog that makes everyone jumpy

Wacky—a dog that has lost its marbles

Walrus—an overweight dog

Wiggles—a dog whose whole body shakes

Yahoo—a dog you are always calling because it won't listen

Yosemite—a dog that loves to roam in the mountains

Zombie—a dog that sleeps a lot

RIDICULOUS DOG RIDDLES

Question: What kind of dog is made of canvas?
Answer: *A pup tent.*

Question: Why do dogs bury bones in the ground?
Answer: *Because they can't bury them in trees.*

Question: Why did the poor dog chase his own tail?
Answer: *He was trying to make both ends meet.*

Question: Why do dogs wag their tails?
Answer: *Because no one else will do it for them.*

Question: Why didn't the dog speak to his foot?
Answer: *Because it's not polite to talk back to your paw.*

"No thanks, I already have every
room in my house alarmed."

Question: Who is a dog's favorite comedian?
Answer: *Growl-cho Marx.*

Question: What did the cowboy say when a
bear ate Lassie?
Answer: *"Well, doggone!"*

Question: What happened when the dog went
to the flea circus?
Answer: *He stole the show.*

Question: How can you tell if you have a stupid
dog?
Answer: *It chases parked cars.*

Question: What kind of dog can use the
phone?
Answer: *A dial-matian*

Question: What kind of dog would you find in
a cave?
Answer: *A bat terrier*

Question: What did the hungry dalmatian say
after his meal?
Answer: *"That hit the spots!"*

"I *think* it's a dog."

Question: Why are dalmatians no good at hide-and-seek?

Answer: *They're always spotted.*

Question: What dog will laugh at any joke?

Answer: *A chi-ha-ha.*

Question: Where do the dogs go for the Macy's Thanksgiving parade?

Answer: *New yorkie.*

Question: What's black and white and red all over?

Answer: *An embarrassed dalmatian.*

Question: How do you catch a runaway dog?

Answer: *Hide behind a tree and make a noise like a bone.*

Question: What dog loves to take bubble baths?

Answer: *A shampoodle.*

Question: What kind of dog does a vampire prefer?

Answer: *A bloodhound.*

Question: What dogs are best for sending tele-
grams?
Answer: *Wire-haired terriers.*

Question: What do you call a happy Lassie?
Answer: *A jolly collie.*

Question: What do you call a nutty dog in Aus-
tralia?
Answer: *A dingo-ling.*

Question: Which dog is good to eat?
Answer: *A hot dog.*

Question: Which side of a dog has the most
hair?
Answer: *The outside.*

Question: Who gave the dog a black eye?
Answer: *Nobody gave it to him. He had to
fight for it.*

Question: Why did the dog go to the doctor
after a tomato fell on his head?
Answer: *The tomato was in a can.*

"Pet Limbo"

Question: Why did the dog jump off the roof of a theater in New York?

Answer: *He wanted to make a hit on Broadway.*

Question: Why did the dog jump up and down in the potato patch?

Answer: *He was growing mashed potatoes.*

Question: Why did the dog mistake the dog catcher for a grape?

Answer: *He was color-blind.*

Question: Why did the dog run around in circles?

Answer: *He was a watchdog and needed winding.*

Question: Why did the dog say he was an actor?

Answer: *His leg was in a cast.*

Question: What kind of meat do you give a stupid dog?

Answer: *Chump chops.*

"He ate my homework and
now he has bookworms."

Question: What does a pet dog wear?

Answer: *A pet-ticoat.*

Question: Why did the dachshund bite the woman's ankle?

Answer: *Because he was short and couldn't reach any higher.*

Question: Why did the snowman call his mean dog Frost?

Answer: *Because Frost bites.*

Question: Where does a rottweiler sit in the cinema?

Answer: *Anywhere it wants to.*

Question: What did the angry man sing when he found his slippers chewed up by the new puppy?

Answer: *"I must throw that doggie out the window..."*

Question: Why did the dog wear white sneakers?

Answer: *Because his boots were at the shoe repair shop.*

"Have you tried walking around in quick
circles right before going to sleep?"

"He's a different kind of boxer."

Question: When is a stray dog most likely to walk into your house?

Answer: *When the door is open.*

Question: What happens when it rains cats and dogs?

Answer: *You can step in a poodle.*

Question: What do you call a sick dog?

Answer: *A germy shepherd.*

Question: What do you sing while bathing your dog?

Answer: *"Working at the dog wash..."*

Question: Where do you find a dog with no legs?

Answer: *Right where you left him.*

Question: Old Mother Hubbard went to the cupboard to get her poor dog a bone, but when she opened it, what letters did she find?

Answer: *M and T.*

Question: What are a dog's favorite pizza toppings?

Answer: *Pup-peroni and mutt-zarella.*

Question: What do you call a dog lying in the sun?

Answer: *A hot dog.*

Question: Why is it better to have a tree in your house than a dog?

Answer: *Because its bark will not bother the neighbors.*

Question: What's more amazing than a talking dog?

Answer: *A spelling bee.*

Question: What do you call a great dog detective?

Answer: *Sherlock Bones.*

Question: What do you call a dog called Bob?

Answer: *Bob.*

Question: What did the puppy say when he sat on some sandpaper?

Answer: *Ruff.*

Question: How does a dog stop a DVD?

Answer: *He presses the paws button.*

"Ready for your bath, big fella?"

Question: What did Rover say when he sat on top of his doghouse?

Answer: *"Roof! Roof!"*

Question: What dogs make the best librarians?

Answer: *Hush puppies.*

Question: What kind of dog sounds like you can eat it?

Answer: *A wiener dog.*

Question: What do you do if your dog eats your pen?

Answer: *Use a pencil instead.*

Question: What do dogs have that no other animal has?

Answer: *Puppies.*

Question: What is a dog's favorite sport?

Answer: *Formula-one drooling.*

Question: What is a dog's favorite food?

Answer: *Anything that is on your plate.*

Question: What dog wears contact lenses?

Answer: *A cock-eyed spaniel.*

Question: What is a dog's favorite flower?
Answer: *Anything in your garden.*

Question: What's a dog favorite hobby?
Answer: *Collecting fleas.*

Question: How many seasons are there in a dog's life?
Answer: *Just one—the shedding season.*

Question: Why is it called a "litter" of puppies?
Answer: *Because they mess up the whole house.*

Question: How do you stop a dog from smelling?
Answer: *Put a cork in its nose.*

Question: What is the best time to take a rottweiler for a walk?
Answer: *Any times he wants to.*

Question: When does a dog say "moo"?
Answer: *When it's learning a new language.*

"If you were really loyal,
you wouldn't be suing me!"

Question: What kind of dog chases anything red?

Answer: *A bulldog.*

Question: What kind of dog wears a uniform and medals?

Answer: *A guard dog.*

Question: What do you call a dog in jeans and a sweater?

Answer: *A plainclothes police dog.*

Question: What do you call a dog in the middle of a muddy road?

Answer: *A mutt in a rut.*

Question: When is a black dog not a black dog?

Answer: *When it's a greyhound.*

Question: What did the dog say when he was attacked by an alligator?

Answer: *Nothing. Dogs can't talk.*

Question: What would you do if a large, fierce dog charged you?

Answer: *Pay him cash.*

Question: What happened to the dog that swallowed the watch?

Answer: *He got ticks.*

Question: Why did the Saint Bernard cross the street?

Answer: *To slobber on the other side.*

Question: What's the difference between a barking dog and an umbrella?

Answer: *You can shut the umbrella up.*

Question: Why are dogs like hamburger?

Answer: *They're both sold by the pound.*

Question: What do dogs order in restaurants?

Answer: *French flies.*

Question: What do you give a dog with a fever?

Answer: *Mustard. It's the best thing for a hot dog.*

Question: What do you say to a dog before he eats?

Answer: *"Bone appetite."*

"It might help Skippy's feelings
if you said he needed improvement instead
of calling him a bad dog."

Question: What do you call a group of very boring, spotted dogs?

Answer: *101 dull-matians.*

Question: What do you call mad pests on a dog?

Answer: *Looney-tics.*

Question: What do you call a dog with bananas in its ears?

Answer: *Anything. He can't hear you.*

Question: What's bright blue, very large, and very heavy?

Answer: *A Great Dane holding its breath.*

Question: What did the dog do when he couldn't afford to buy a new car?

Answer: *He leashed one.*

Question: What do you give a dog to make him laugh?

Answer: *A funny bone.*

Question: What does a dog take with him when he interviews a gorilla?

Answer: *An ape recorder.*

"I'm wagging my tail on the outside,
but I'm whimpering on the inside.

Question: Where do dogs and cats go to get their prescriptions filled?

Answer: *Old MacDonald's farm-acy.*

Question: What animal goes "Baa-Baa-Woof"?

Answer: *A sheepdog.*

Question: What is the difference between a dog and a marine scientist?

Answer: *One wags a tail, the other tags a whale.*

Question: When is a dog's tail not a dog's tail?

Answer: *When it is a waggin'.*

Question: What would you get if you crossed a noisy frog and a shaggy dog?

Answer: *A croaker spaniel.*

Question: What do they call a dog at the United Nations?

Answer: *A diplo-mutt.*

Question: Where do they send homeless dogs?

Answer: *To the arf-anage.*

Question: What spot would a bloodhound get in *Hollywood Squares?*

Answer: *The scenter square.*

Question: What would you get if you crossed a peach with a pooch?

Answer: *A pit bull.*

Question: What would you get if you crossed a cartoon dog with a doctor who talks to the animals?

Answer: *Dr. Scooby-Doo-Little.*

Question: What would you get if you crossed an angry dog with a lobster?

Answer: *A Doberman pincher.*

Question: What kind of dog keeps an eye on the kids?

Answer: *A baby-setter.*

Question: What has four legs, is furry, and goes, "Foow, Foow"?

Answer: *A dog chasing a car in reverse.*

Question: What is the snootiest dog?

Answer: *A cocky spaniel.*

Question: Where do you look for a missing dog?

Answer: *At the lost-a-hound pound.*

Question: Where do you buy fresh dog biscuits?

Answer: *At a barkery.*

Question: What do performing dogs do after the show?

Answer: *Take a bow-wow.*

Question: Why do fire trucks have dogs on them?

Answer: *To find the fire hydrant.*

Question: What do you call a dog that likes to bake cakes?

Answer: *Betty Cocker.*

Question: What does a dog say when it gets sick?

Answer: *"Barf. Barf."*

Question: How are dog catchers paid?

Answer: *By the pound.*

"Do you think rolling over will
be on the finals?"

Question: What kind of arguments do dogs like at dinner?
Answer: *Table scraps.*

Question: What two dogs are opposites?
Answer: *Hot dogs and chili dogs.*

Question: If every dog has its day, what does a dog with a broken tail have?
Answer: *A weekend.*

Question: Who brings dogs their presents at Christmas?
Answer: *Santa Paws.*

Question: What kind of dog washes clothes?
Answer: *A laundro-mutt.*

Question: What has no hair and thinks it's the national dog of the United States?
Answer: *The bald beagle.*

Question: What is a dog's favorite soup?
Answer: *Chicken poodle.*

"Oh, great," thought the wolf,
"a border collie."

"It looks like he got up on the
wrong side of the bed again."

Question: What do you call the top of a dog-house?

Answer: *The woof.*

Question: What's worse than a dog howling at the moon?

Answer: *Two dogs howling at the moon.*

Question: Which breed of dogs eats with its tail?

Answer: *All dogs keep their tails on when eating.*

Question: How did the dog feel when he lost his flashlight?

Answer: *Delighted.*

Question: What happened when the dog fell into a lens-grinding machine?

Answer: *He made a spectacle of himself.*

Question: What would you do if you found an angry pit bull in your kitchen?

Answer: *Eat out.*

"It's part of his community service."

Question: What would you do if you found an angry pit bull asleep on your bed?

Answer: *Sleep on the sofa.*

Question: What would you do if you found an angry pit bull wearing your favorite tie?

Answer: *Go see a psychiatrist. You've been seeing entirely too many angry pit bulls lately.*

Question: What did the dog do when he broke his toe?

Answer: *He called a toe truck.*

Question: How do you keep a dog from barking in your front yard?

Answer: *Put him in the backyard.*

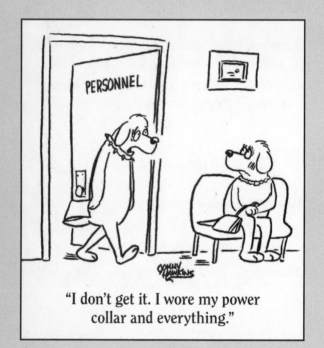

"I don't get it. I wore my power
collar and everything."

SLED DOG RIDDLES

Question: How can you tell if you have a stupid sled dog?

Answer: *It chases parked snowmobiles.*

Question: What did the sled dogs say when their pizza was delivered?

Answer: *"Arctic hare, lemmings...Hey. Didn't we order puffins on this thing?"*

Question: What do sled dogs say before telling you a joke?

Answer: *"This one will sleigh you."*

Question: Why did the sled dog cross the snow softly?

Answer: *Because it just got hit by a snowmobile and couldn't walk hardly.*

Question: What is the difference between
Santa Claus and a warm sled dog?

Answer: *Santa wears a whole suit—a dog just
pants.*

Question: What did the vet say to the musher
who brought in a sled dog with caribou
steak on its head, seal meat stuffed up its
nose, and lemmings stuck in its ears?

Answer: *"Your dog isn't eating right."*

Question: What do you do when you park your
sled in very cold weather?

Answer: *Plug in your dogs.*

Question: What kind of dog sniffs out new
flowers on the tundra?

Answer: *A bud hound.*

Question: What would you get if you crossed a
puffin with a sled dog?

Answer: *A dog that lays pooched eggs.*

Question: What time is it when ten sled dogs
are chasing a polar bear across the ice?

Answer: *Ten after one.*

Question: What does a sled dog that was an Iditarod competitor become after it is ten years old?

Answer: *Eleven years old.*

Question: How long are a sled dog's legs?

Answer: *All the way down to the snow.*

Question: Where are sled dogs trained?

Answer: *In the mush-room.*

Question: What do you call a litter of young dogs that have come in out of the snow?

Answer: *Slush puppies.*

Question: How did the sled dog make anti-freeze?

Answer: *It ran off with her blanket.*

Question: How is a sled dog like your nose on a cold day?

Answer: *They both run.*

Question: Where do sled dogs go when they've lost their tails?

Answer: *A retail store.*

Question: What do you call a sled dog with no legs?

Answer: *It doesn't matter what you call it—it still won't run.*

Question: How many legs do sled dogs have?

Answer: *Six. Forelegs at the front and two at the back.*

Question: If your sled dog fell through a hole in the ice, what is the first thing it would do?

Answer: *Get wet!*

Question: How many hairs are in a sled dog's tail?

Answer: *None. They're all on the outside.*

Question: How do you make a slow sled dog fast?

Answer: *Don't feed it.*

Question: Why aren't sled dogs good dancers?

Answer: *Because they have two left feet.*

Question: How can you tell if you have a stupid sled dog?

Answer: *There's a long pause after "bow" while it tries to remember "wow."*

Question: How can you tell if you have a stupid sled dog?

Answer: *It buries its tail and wags its bones.*

Question: What's a sign that your sled dog may not be an Iditarod winner?

Answer: *Its collar doubles as its medic alert bracelet.*

Question: What's a sign that your sled dog may not like you?

Answer: *You catch it gnawing on your snowmobile's brake line.*

Question: What's another sign that your sled dog may not like you?

Answer: *Whenever you're having a bath, it decides to fetch electric appliances.*

Question: What do sled dogs play with to amuse themselves?

Answer: *Their Sony Sleigh Station.*

Other Books by Bob Phillips

All-Time Awesome Collection
of Good Clean Jokes for Kids

The Awesome Book
of Bible Trivia

Awesome Good Clean
Jokes for Kids

Awesome Knock-Knock
Jokes for Kids

The Best of the Good
Clean Jokes

Bible Trivia for Every Day

Dude, Got Another Joke?

Extremely Good Clean
Jokes for Kids

Fabulous and Funny
Clean Jokes for Kids

Flat-Out Awesome Knock-Knock
Jokes for Kids

Good Clean Jokes to Drive Your
Parents Crazy

Good Clean Knock-Knock
Jokes for Kids

Jolly Jokes for Older Folks

Nutty Knock-Knock
Jokes for Kids

Over the Hill & On a Roll

Over the Next Hill
& Still Rolling

Over the Top Clean
Jokes for Kids

Super Incredible Knock-Knock
Jokes for Kids

The World's Greatest
Collection of Clean Jokes

The World's Greatest
Knock-Knock Jokes for Kids

Other Books by Bob Phillips
and Jonny Hawkins

The Awesome Book
of Cat Humor

The Awesome Book
of Heavenly Humor

A Joke a Day Keeps
the Doctor Away

Laughter from
the Pearly Gates

Other Books by Jonny Hawkins

Fishing Cartoon-a-Day Calendar

Medical Cartoon-a-Day Calendar

Car 'Toon-a-Day Calendar